My Ardent Love for the Pencil

Vi Khi Nao

My Ardent Love for the Pencil

ISBN: 978-1-968523-09-1

All photos in this book were taken by the author.

The cover was designed by David Wojciechowsk. Find more of his work at davidwojo.com. We are grateful to Jörn Peter Budesheim for allowing us to use his drawing on the cover. Find more of his work at https://sites.google.com/view/budesheim.

Malarkeybooks.com

For my mother, Ali Raz, and C.D. Wright

How could she be a lesbian when her hair is so straight?

My camera remembers you.

I want to borrow the tranquility of her desire and make it my own.

I tell her, you can't have me but you can have my memory of you.

Maybe one day I will have a video tape of your memory.

I am trying to put my hand as a placeholder in her body—like reading a book—I just want to know what page I am on.

I can't wait for the world to hide her mouth in my purse.

And just like that I let her go.

Wake up, Dreams! Let me give you a bath!
It is just me—I need censorship!

He deflated my penis by taking too long, but I brought a bicycle pump with me.

I offer them my body. I offer them my drama.

When I meet people I learn to collapse time now...so as if I have known them all of my life.

Life doesn't have to be dark when I have friends who care about me.

Nothing can prevent you from the loneliness of an empty room. Or an empty hotel room. Or an empty house.

Vi, I am not attracted to attractive people, says Lela out of the blue.

I know my love for you would come with pain, like a razor blade tucked inside the heart of a rose.

Use our body as an instrument for sound.
I am not here for self-preservation.

I wonder if our relationship is a moped, if it doesn't stay on the accelerator, it will lose momentum and fall down.

We are superior beings with inferior strength.

We are inferior beings with superior strength.

The two trees shake their leaves to sing sonnets.
You could use your words as a corridor!

Indotoxin

I wish I hadn't told everyone I had a clitoris.

I need to apply for things to get my testimonies of failure.

We are all powerful seahorses that couldn't get our husbands pregnant!

I wouldn't ask you to be faithful to me but wouldn't it be nice for our relationship if you were?

We are ballooned deep in each other. The Snowcone.

Sometimes you need to give money away to feel alive.
I dreamt that Rocco died and he has killed someone.

I love you with the bottomless odor of my existence.

I accidentally spread deodorant on my dental floss and now the armpits of my teeth are complaining!

If I am liquor, you must be languor.

I am in love with stingy people. I follow them around like a baby puppy.

I am losing my sex drive.

With one season in your body, you can bury the snow.

I am thinking of growing chest hair so that the eyes of my nipples would have eyebrows—what kind of mascara should I get?

I don't do darkness anymore & I chase light around a room.

Nepotism is a self-inflicted wound, says Helia Rabie on the publishing industry.

Wisdom from Helia Rabie

"Sad people are stingy," says Helia Rabie. "Diversify your social life. Don't hang out with writers." Helia Rabie Source—find the source You can't manufacture phenomenon. You can't even manufacture passion. Do what you love. Helia thinks Thalia Field is the smartest. Her first impression of Carole was lack of respect. Most of everyone. The princess of Iran who committed suicide three years ago. Wanted to work with Carole. Brian was trying to get Joanna fired, she thought. Helia thinks she is cynical. Conversation with Helia. My eye problems disappear after the MFA was done. It was a toxic environment for Helia. An eye patch. I like the way she thinks I like things that suspend me from this world. Where I am a part of this world but not really. There is a layer of reality. Violinist at an underground station. That could stop my soul from moving forward. You have to admire someone's work properly. Or I would look down upon you for wrongly and inaccurately admiring my work.

Sencha rose tea Bluestocking Strand Isabela Rosselini.

My body is a window against which some girl relaxes her face.

My tears have become disobedient and fall from my eyes like a necklace.

Pencil—I am lying on a minimal bed in Dumbo—thinking of you—of how close I want to be near you.

Come here. Let me microwave your heart with my fear of intimacy.

We all berate each other for our mediocrity.

How do I remove the minds of others from my mind?

It won't be me—I don't love you in the same way.

You trick the heart to lose its mind or to pretend to like something—but you can't make it love what it does not love.

You can't trick the heart into thinking or make the heart deceive itself by mere force or distraction.

I know deep down. So deep down—I want my pencil. With her I feel her at the deepest level of connection. It is too bad—she had evacuated herself from my existence.... It is really too bad.

Who do I want to be intimate with today? Random strangers or my clitoris?

The sound of wind chime waking up another wind chime.
The sound of one chorus waking up another chorus.

I wake up, an image of me in a pencil's arm.

Play idea
Man pours grapefruit juice from a bottle. His roommate goes into the refrigerator and takes the grapefruit container and makes a mark each time he pours it out. And, puts it back in. His roommate comes in, drinks/pours out some. Much later, he comes back with a new grapefruit bottle and pours some of it to refill it. He over refills it and his grapefruit owner roommate ponders how does grapefruit grow from itself. As, it does grow from itself. He pours enough so that it meets the line where he makes it.

Drawing ideas
Man holding his beer bottle penis while his lover uncorks the cap with a beer opener. His nipples are hollowed and replaced with empty beer bottles with the beer bottles facing the viewer.

Each day I interact with my pencil—the more I appreciate her. The subtle things she says or does.

Anything is possible if we share a pillow especially if I don't sleep with a pillow!

I haven't let a dick inside me since 2009 and I haven't been constipated since 2007.

Sometimes a sign of things going bad when it is going too well!

Title for a future book
The novelist is a novel

Can you know someone by merely looking at her across time? From the point of view of your mind?

I don't ask a lot from men—just that they get naked for my book. I don't know much about men's undergarments in fashion—I just think poetry collection, The Old Philosopher, would make a really good boxer or bra.

There is sadness in her truth.

Because we are so passionate, it seems sometimes the only way to channel our creativity is to put it all in the poetic or literary work....because if we don't put it there we suffocate the people we care a great deal about. We put so much soil on top of the flower that is trying to bloom...but to put it all in the literary work....it gets so unbearably lonely too. Between two lonelinesses—the loneliness of creating and the loneliness of suffocating, which loneliness would you choose?

But the best kind of love is the one that allows us to be ourselves, angelic and neurotic without being psychotic. And take us for who we are. Without condemnation. Without judgement.

Novel

About a woman who wants to lean into a tree and dies but each step she takes she is being interrupted by the vibrant, slow, unconscious ruler around her.

A waste of human poetic space to not turn love making into the highest form of performance art.

The poetic space of fucking exists not in the ritual but in the risk of vulnerability.

When my pencil lingers and reciprocates my gaze, when she does that I realize I could, in a glimpse, understand the infrastructure of infinity.

The initial gaze. I am studying the way the pencil gazes at me. I am studying the wind. When she holds my gaze, there is power there. Followed by the flickering of pleasure between the perceptual mind and the perceptual cunt, which throbs or flickers in unison between my heart and my cunt and my mind's cunt like light inside of the kerosene lamp. The small wind that rushes forward. Trembles. The pencil gazes at me as if she is surrendering herself. I gaze back at her knowing that my insides have not been the same.

My desire for the pencil

It was hard to tell if she would be awake for our 3 a.m. encounter on top of her roof. It wasn't as if my desire for her were a t-shirt at a laundromat where she expects me to wear it inside out. I had come to her with an unshakable longing. Wanting the pencil ahead of time. Sitting in my consciousness, waiting for the hour to forestall itself. Waiting for the bathroom to open itself, waiting for the window to close itself. Yet, it took me an hour and half from East Harlem on the 1:30 a.m. night train for me to arrive to the pencil's backyard: a notepad that hasn't been written on before.

Dia wakes up with the revelation that she wants to be rich. So she could have a washer and dryer in her apartment.

Invisible sentences—if you come to me again I will murder you.

She is sad that I sent her friend, the pen, into exile.

There are things on your body that are harder than mountains and travel faster than snow.

There are things in this world, faster than demons, faster than roses.

The way you were lying flat—there were obvious snowstorms on your body.

It's obvious I am addressing the pencil.

Poetry accepted my two poems!! After seven years of submitting, they finally saw the light of the day.

Your beauty is all over you. You don't need surface to dictate your beauty.

Technologyless in the presence of others.

1. Baking: Poet's face lying in the sand 2. Open:

eyes opening 3. Red: A red ball passes over my face in slow motion / cloth pulling over the frame / face and the screen is red 4. Feasting: feasting of steam from a block of ice / an animal feasting / a table of food / no humans / laying the table with an apple in the poet's mouth 5. Eyeslonging: a needle, eye of the needle, elongating the length of the needle 6. Musky: the belly of log lifting in the wood or film the barrel you make the manhattan, back of knees 7. Blue: a translucent jar or a wine bottle and then we have blue cloth and lower that cloth into the mouth of the jar / wine bottle / jar containing blue fluid. 8. Prairie: put or tape grass in a jar, enclosed natural world 9. Standing: poet just standing in despair 10. Body: taping upper parts of the poet's body from pages of a book 11. Oven: image of poet wearing a makeshift skirt and an oven 12. A river, water flowing and taking the turn like a knee 13. Sucking: vacuum cleaner, get the vacuum cleaner sucking up grass, snow, soil, dessert, cloth, olive, or a fruit, gopro: underwater filming of a vacuum cleaner sucking up an olive or a piece of cloth or something fruity 14. Dry: sucking up sand 15. Around: hand wrapping a rope, or wrapping a gift, gripping a banister 16.

Clavicle: filming the poet's clavicle 17. Necklace: droplet of water on poet's neck 18. Roaring: water, filming waves coming in 19. Kiss: two leaves to touch one another 20. Cycle: salad spinnet, dough mixture 21. Hush: baby sleeping, finger on lip, quiet, leaves rustling on trees 22. Time: someone walking backward 23. Buried: t-shirt crumpled and tossed into pillowcase and pressed down, flour sack, dough tossed and pressed down 24. Undulating: horse's back 25. Exile: pages falling in a corner or dough left in the corner to rise 26. Hold: hand gripping flour sack by neck 27. Fat: bacon on sand, sizzling bacon 28. Rain: something related to rain 29. Meat: bacon, wrapped around dough 30. Thick: crust of bread, rim of it 31. Lift: shirt lifted from a blender or dough machine 32. Timer: clock, blocks of number and toss them on a pile of flour 33. Naked: nude back, a bread cut, a piece of fruit being peeled, avocado 34. Rubbing: 35. Motion: baking sheet in motion 36. Knot, two ropes tugging at each other 37. Kernel: corn, bread, two plants fucking, donut and something 38. Tight: rope tightening around the flesh of dough 39. Thighs: two baguettes rising 40. Nipples: two raspberries on the two pieces of breast-shaped dough 41. Divisions: divide bread into portions 42. Grass: toss dough on grass 43. Weight: tossing two doughs on top of each other 44. Thrusting: pounding of knuckles into dough 45. Hand: four hands piling on top of each other 46. Pussy: introduction of two cats, pussy willow 47. Interlaced: strips of dough interlaced with strips of dough 48. Crescent: use a baking tool to arch the back of a leaf or a plant 49. Flour: toss flour into a metal bowl, powder fluff up 50. River: water running out if faucet 51. Heat: dough onto desert 52. Orgasm: explosion inside dough, champagne 53. 53.

Aiska is very late

When he rode me in his motorcycle, The wind shook my face like a glass of water When I climbed down from the bike My face spilled all over me

My river is a reflection on my river

When you hang out with people too much, you can lose your moral compass.

If I want a flat diet coke, I will go for a guy!!

Film idea:
a man who sits in a restaurant and sobs for half an hour while life passes by

The building blocks of torture

Advertising idea:
sexy male nude—holding The Old Philosopher.

You can't get lazy when it comes to love. You just can't.

If a duck eats several aqueducts each year, what would a vi be doing if not eating several viaducts each year too?

Tear me away from my symbol of light.

Your consciousness has been burning a will in your body.

Think really hard about what you want, Vi. What if you want nothing. It is okay to want nothing.

I feel so sad and vulnerable.

I tried to fix myself by being myself, allowing me to be me, but there is something very fucked up about this. I kept on thinking of my pen, and how when she was still alive, I had desire to keep on going, pursuing things, advancing my place in the publishing world. I thought of the time when I had arrived to Providence. I don't remember how I arrived there, but the pen said she would meet me. Without asking if I needed my luggage carried, she impressively advanced towards my wheeled suitcase, wheeled it to her Toyota hybrid, and lifted the entire luggage with 10 of my books and clothes into the trunk. She turned to me, "I am scrawny like a tree, but strong and sturdy." I believed every word of it. She knew I couldn't lift and had been lifting a lot during my travel and wanted to lighten the load for me. When I entered her car, the tears I held in nearly spilled out of me like beans and they were in the midst of running away from me. I knew this even when she hugged me and told me that she loved me.

This pencil.

Each day I imagine cuddling with a pencil and when cuddling with a pencil didn't work out, I imagined cuddling with a pen. And soon, my entire existence began to shut down. And, each time it shut down, I felt so tired and burnt out. Not like a candle near the end of its wax, but like a pot of broth without any broth left and the burner kept on burning. And, my mind was sitting on the floor of the kitchen, scraping the burnt off. I had been in this state for months, even years. I found writing so repulsive that I wondered if I would ever recover and be normal like everyone else, sexual creatures of this earth with still living sexual and emotional desire. I wondered how long I was going to be this way? The thought of dying alone didn't seem to make me flinch. What made me flinch was the return of feeling nothing. A little dead inside that seemed a lot.

Is your orgasm geopolitical? Find out by reading my poetry collection, *The Old Philosopher*.

It is just me and darkness.

I vacillate between overworking or loneliness. Endless time to myself bathing in the soiled light of solitude. I wish that I had desired the same desire as my peers—but it seems I want the kind of pleasure that comes with time and posterity.

The worst thing I could do to myself is to become complacent

Review for Sid
You can tell from reading the book that the writer (s) gallivants and, in writing and on foot, covers much geographical and intellectual territories. The book is surprisingly perennial and it gives you the illusion that time passes through mankind while not quite passing through. There are stories of time—nonhuman time—that behave more like childlike parables, not meant to be taken seriously...though there are other vagrant stories that are deeply embedded in the motion of wisdom—these stories take time to reveal themselves. I hope you will have the pleasure of reading it—the writer is obviously very meticulous.

"They fetishized themselves." -Tania

How easily you can endanger
The night with your words and silhouettes.

An unshakable sadness penetrates me.

A young man is pursuing my mother. My mother is 20 years older than him. They are having an unquiet conversation over OKCupid. She asks him, why are you seeking a woman on the verge of falling asleep with death? He replies, "Older women are like apples high up on an apple tree. You have to climb higher up, risking and breaking your legs for them. The apples closer to the ground are easier to pick, but I don't want those apples."

Domestic lives made eerie by their lack of eeriness.

She has been so agitated lately. Everything turned her into coals. She couldn't extinguish. Why wouldn't he add more photos into his Instagram account? He kept on liking her posts. Sometimes he liked all five of her uploaded photographs. Sometimes he liked most of what she brought to the new digital table. He would like her posts. He was an exempt. Today he liked one more of her banal posts. It was a picture of a dismantled snowflake. Sugar melting. She made a small, unconstrained scream inside her body. Why wouldn't he add more photos? Agitated, she impulsively deleted him off her account. Except he would still be able to like her photos, while she was completely prevented and occluded from liking his photos. She would have to add him back on or beg him to add her. She had no choice but to dislike him. She knew he was a type of comforter that absorbed too much smoke.

I think the primary problem with my writing is that I use too many words.

Design is a large part of writing *Fish in Exile*.

I made shrimp egg drop soup with firm tofu and tomatoes for my mother.

I am glad I am not teaching. It will make me too human and the kind of writing I want to do, I can't be human in order to do them.

Is this the year to kill oneself?

This is my mother and her attempt at the obvious.

Tearing my hair out from filing bankruptcy papers for my mother.

Dear God, I need your help. Will you help me make my poetry collection, *The Old Philosopher*, the number 1 best seller in the New York Times and my novel, *Fish In Exile*, as well. I don't know how to make this happen. I would love some guidance. Your other god, Vi

I want to tell him that he does not understand my heart because if he understood he wouldn't ask me this question.

dear matt~ i attempt at
this it is bad isn't
it? 2.23.2026

His wealth makes you poor and makes him poor as well.

Most women's clitorises are being born to inspire birth or pleasure, but it seems mine is born to fall asleep during a thunderstorm.

Whenever I think of being in an intimate relationship, I shut down. I turn towards you to fill a void in me.

Is there disease in the wind? Is there time in my silhouette?

Tomorrow when my footsteps grow old.

Please take me home to kiss me goodnight.

Mother of ruin. Father of despair. Please kiss me goodnight.

La Noche

If the night dies, let me die with the night
And if my shadow doesn't grow old,
Take my breath to sea and bury it next to the skyline
If the night dies, let me kiss you goodnight

5 or 6

Ranking order of blurbers Joanna Ruocco Rae Armantrout 4 months (may 2017) Book Forum Raintaxi New York Times Advanced Review Copies ARCs After been published Literary magazines Quarterly List of reviewers (personal copies) Prize money (not royalty) No advance on regular pub Fc2 not UA press Prior publication Acknowledgment No signed publications Author questionnaire Dedication Let the designer try the cover Release to photographer University of Pitts. Northwestern Iowa presses.

Don't eviscerate me, world.

One time he felt down and shattered his toilet into pieces. I wondered if his body inadvertently felt the pain and bruising became as a result and reminder of being abused by his mother in his youth who beat him and living in the same household where his father repeatedly raped his sisters. Did he become overtly corpulent, an extra layer of insulin, to protect him from this world? His body seemed like visual testimonies of his past and it seemed that the only way to know that he was alive and to have this unshakable past was to allow his body to re-enter the unbreakable hemisphere of the ever returning insulin injections, injuries, bruises, accidents. But abuses of the mind and body were never an accident. They were out of the cycle of not knowing how to transform.

When you use your body as
A gun

Human embrace. Is it like making cheese? Double boiler. A pot inside of a pot. Why are goat's breasts so long. Are you jealous yours are not that elongated? I asked my mother. My mother's culinary exlover used to milk 200 to 300 cows each morning. They used to look at him kindly. Brine 2 cups whey, two cups of salt. Four cups of water.

For the Member

They attempted at a coup, but each attempt landed them in jail and their ration pulled back. Their starvation state increased to an utter state of despair. So when they were imprisoned, loaves of bread and fish were teleported to them. The commanders of the prisons were confused at the state of their prisoners' well being. They couldn't understand why the prisoners were not emaciated. They did not understand why they were not starving. They didn't understand the fish bones left in the corner of their prison wall. They did not understand how the prisoners had access to food.

Kevin helped my mother put up new curtains

I dreamt of water. Lots of water. A huge wave came crashing. After a demonstration of needle and thread. For a book binding. The water came rushing and rushing. Most of the swimmers made it through the great water rush. But I remained dormant under water from March to August. Before emerging from the depth of water. I kept on asking everyone why I was able to stay underwater for so long. I kept on asking how did they know where to look for my un-submersion. Where to greet and retrieve me. One person discloses that they came out each day to the same spot to wait for me.

I wouldn't mind dying right now. I wouldn't mind passing away in my sleep.

I slept on the floor for months and couldn't afford a bed, but in the midst of it all, I prepared an interview for Notre Dame. Only to find out a month later some white dude got it. He would probably get it even if he didn't show up for his own presentation.

Writing letter to Giovan at mother's sewing table/machine

Letter to Tania

I had a dream about my pencil. She was sitting next to me at a backless table. She reminded me to not mix the word desert with dessert in a catalogue for my book. She sat so close to me. Her body right up to my body. She was wearing a dress, dark, I think. It may have sequins. After she reminded me to punctuate correctly, she sat next to me, without leaving. I could feel her woody warm body and it sparked all forms of desire in me. I wanted to pull her out of my pencil holder. The muscular softness of her sitting next to me made me want her more and more. I did not have to pull her into my arms due to the closeness of her proximity. We sat there, so tightly close, for a lingering long time. Because of the pencil's lingering stay, I wonder perhaps if she was reciprocating my desire for her.

Lisa after eight years

General Westmoreland
Lisa's father. George Neary. Lieutenant.

Karma
You carry your past inside you. Without knowing what you have carried.

Berta Caceres, Honduras environment and human rights activist, murdered.

Each cup of tears sits on each cup of tears.

Storage (journal/heater/clothes) Post office Drop books off at Prairie Lights Schedule reading time at Prairie Lights Stuff to collect furniture Text adam Deposit $60

Not with the knife to my heart.

I prefer to be imperfect and have that work be my own than to have perfection and not my own. Unless it is collaboration.

We relapse into micro-neuroses of assholeness, but Cd was purposeful in her kindness. It is impossible for humans to be kind all the time. It exhausted us.

I gaze inwardly for my sorrow. I gaze outwardly for tomorrow. I gaze at myself without gazing at myself and this is where the knife of the presence kills me.

I think cinema mirrors life a bit more than literature. This is why we welcome the world of fiction. How many frames per second can the human eyes see? When we gaze back at the memories of our past, we do not see that half of our memories should exist in the darkness to reflect the times when the sun goes down on us. And half of our memories bathing in light to emulate the diurnal condition of the time the sun rises upon us. But we don't remember our past this way, in terms of memory. We remember the past in still frames or in one continuous flow.

When we rewind the pages or passages of cinema, we see that we do watch its world half in darkness. There are thirty frames per second. To study one minute of this Sheep Machine, it requires the scrutiny of 1800 frames or 30×60, since it is quite clear here that there are 60 seconds in a minute. Has memory permitted you to gaze at your past or future in such a micro level? Cinema has the ability to do this.

Let me access your soul and allow you to access mine as I attempt to showcase as many media as possible.

From Carole, "An autopsy was done, but no results are back yet. oh Vi—is this not the saddest sentence in the world? My hunch is that she had arrhythmia. I learned that about a month ago she fainted and could not be revived. The doctors in Providence did nothing...Don't get me started.

There will be a gathering for grad students probably on the 27th just so we can mourn together probably at the Granoff, and a formal memorial somewhere down the line. I will keep you posted. Where are you?"

For the Member

The boy is trying to convince his mother not to commit suicide after she stuffed banh mi into her body to store the food for them, but he also wants to commit suicide too.

I work hard at not censoring my protagonists.

Try to sterilize or vaccinate the language.

No one wants to talk about the liminal space between wanting something and the journey it takes to acquire it.

You should view the novel to a music score or a piece of music: moving through different moods. It should be fluid and raw.

The novel itself does not come into the world to mock or give birth to realism or to play into character. It is only faithful to a philosophy that births it. It is driven by moods, textual, sexual, sonic ontological moods.

The work gives no pretense that it attempts to be a long narrative piece.

The device of intimacy is also used to make the text aware of itself.

Here Ethos is clearing the throat of his dialogue based existence. It should be awkward and it should not conform to the play-formatting that is used throughout the rest of the novel. It is okay at this moment that his name isn't attached to any colons.

Consistency for consistency's sake I do not want.

If my text happens to experience an orgasm, it was not born to but was made to.

Repetition is also a device of foreplay. It rubs the clitoris of the text over and over again to subliminally titillate it. It builds desire and yearning and wants. It is a text that has an active sex life. And, ultimately the protagonists climax and so does the text.

A way for language to be aware of itself without being blatantly aware of itself. Poetry in context of a novel can be used as a rhetoric device for language to be hyperaware of itself: extreme poetic gestures as seen in the interaction between Ethos and Catholic at times give the illusion that the text does not belong there, but it does. Some observe that the language is too flowery and at times too beautiful for it and makes the text too self-conscious of itself. This is true. The text and its author won't deny this. Stage direction borrowed from plays also allow language to know itself, be hyperaware of itself. In this way I am using stage direction as another layer of metafiction. This is not only a style choice but also a philosophical choice. Metafiction in the 21st does not give pretense that it is not what it is not. It blatantly declares itself as being meta. I am here to impose my existence on the text. It wants to say. My metafiction uses various devices outside of the novel to talk to its own text and being somewhat remarkably sly with it. When this does happen, the text itself appears either awkward, comedic, or imposingly poetic. The language here purposefully does not pretend to blend itself into the text and the text should not attempt to be colloquial because in its poetic pose, it has adapted to a new register by acquiring a new shape-shifting vernacular without asking the permission from the readers if this is okay for it to do so. It does it anyway. The readers should not see this gesture as betraying the emotional or intellectual core of the entire work, but as an act of pure betrayal. This new kind of betrayal is necessary for the vitality of the text. As change cannot happen without this kind of betrayal. Repetition is another metafiction device I use frequently for text to acknowledge itself. While I have used repetition to build erotic pulses throughout the body of the text to give it electrical energy, its enigma lies in the repetition's device of manipulating time. While repetition may be seen as wasting time and words, repeating something that has already been said already or appears already been understood, the device itself allows time skipping or time passing or time lagging. If we see repetition as possessing a corporeality, it would take shape as a time machine. When used wisely and precisely and timely, it has the ability to move text in and out of the future and from the past into a fluid present. It has the ability to make language time travel through the different registers. Repetition can move the text telekinetically. And give us the deja vu feeling that we have been there and here already. Repetition is also important in the theoretic treatment of grief and of exile and expulsion. If grief and exile and expulsion force a person to time travel emotionally and geographically time travel, I don't know what is. Grief is a time traveling device. It is a state of being that allow humans to have access to various portals of the subconscious. Until humans develop a less histrionic method to access the ontological experience, grief is one ticket (it is not the only ticket) that Charon will take or allow us to travel from one world to the next. The Chicago Style of Manual, while useful in creating clarity and economy of the sentence, at times I feel its usage sterilize and stifle the text. I try to preserve the poetic language of the text as much as possible to adhere to my metafictional take of the text.

I work hard at not censoring my protagonists. I allow them to be who they are on the page. I try not to remain faithful to realism. It saddens me that you do not understand my work.

Our superhuman skills and ideas of aliens come from the bible. Jesus gave science fiction ideas how to manifest science fiction.

My sadness is unrelenting.

Being so poor financially changed me so much.

Crepuscular light, differentiate yourself from the womb of being.

Maybe in time what was born yesterday will be born today.

Writers do not shower or something. Like they think not showering made them produce great literature or something.

You don't know how dead you are based on the things you dreamt you might have wanted.

Pencil: your heart beats against my womb. Am I doomed?

Things Tania likes : coffee, parks, sleep, the pencil

My body is a finger that points at the rectum of you loving me
There is no outlet for the way I have been loving you. Which is
a disease of Marc-Antoine Matthieu Frank King Andy Bleck

From CD

Vi -
There's no academic job in sight for self-published titles and
these people know the small press world - they are at the dead
center
of it. Recall those titles. Send PDFs of forthcoming books from
Nightboat and Coffee House, both wonderful books.
I need a CV from you. I thought I had written a letter but I just
wrote a blurb.
You are profoundly talented, smart, and dear, but you don't
have time
to get in your own way.
Love,
C.D.

Vi - I have to wait until tomorrow to finish your letter - I need to
review your student teaching evaluations - so I can say something
particular in reference to them - I think I would elaborate a bit
on your work experience - whatever it may be - you can make
it sound interesting - because you're interesting - I want to help
you get your cv up to reflect your actual level of accomplishment
 - you have to stop writing
long enough to pay attention to things such as what to publications
to send the work - i.e., i threw out every glimmer train in

the random library in the lounge becasue they are so lousy -
and to register the wonderful fact that you're multi-lingual -

and I have to stop lecturing you -
later,
c

from c.d.

I delete spam regularly - I will scan my e-mails -
old miss is a moniker for u of miss -
I've never been to oxford but hear it is a good town -
i have a sort of friend - in that i've only met her once but we
are related through friends - who is an anthropologist there -
it is a small town as you know - with a famously good bookstore -
and faulkner's house -
it is difficult to apply for a job in the site where you live -
esp in academia which doesn't cater to "locals" -
even more so if you have a love relationship that doesn't
work out - and more so yet if it's a small town - this goes without
saying -
no? you are innocent - but
you know these things don't you vi -
you know these things - the world is little and bigoted and
unforgiving -
but you can still turn it into whirling daffodils of words -
that's your gift -

Oops - now I see - I'll write it tomorrow - is the position
for fiction or poetry - or hybrid -

if it's hybrid it would be good to submit both - if it's fiction -
just submit fiction - fiction folks don't want
to know or care if you're a poet -
in fact it could be a strike -
probably not in this instance (but this is rare) given the people who
are there -
cd

vi- looking over your cv - you landed good presses for yours mss.
but you never to be more selective in sending out your work to
magazines - there are for better magazines -hundreds of them -
and you can get in them -
i don't really have time to tell you now - i don't have time to write
for any of these publications myself now - and i don't pay attention
to the best magazines for fiction - except maybe Conjunctions
(which
has a "theme" for each issue so you have to look up to see what it
is to know whether you have something that fits); The White Review
(which may be only online but it is very prominent - think it's based
in London), McSweeney's (for fiction and to lesser extent for
poetry - I quit sending there after the poetry editor solicited from
me repeatedly and only accepted once) - The New Republic (not
really a poetry journal but fearsome Cathy Park Hong is poetry ed),
Poor Claudia, Tin House, Lana Turner (an annual).
Look at the credits in the books you care about. That's the company
you want to be in.
Re: your cv again - how many languages do you have. Put that on
your cv. Add whether you are proficient or not - in spoken and in
written
forms.
Have to go.
C

Vi- I don't know how you proceed -
dinner wars part fun part fiasco - the wee one
in the bunch had a meltdown -
anyway - I'll get your letter written tomorrow -
I don't know how you are to proceed anyway -
with respect to interfolio - you submit the names
and people write the letters - cd

Vi-
It's not a stigma to self publish - it's a time-honored tradition -
it just doesn't fly for jobs in college teaching.
Don't send more than more ms. to a single publisher. When you
send a swarm of mss. editors think it already spells trouble
for them. And it "presents" as graphomania.
Sorry, shorthand explanation. Have guests coming over.
Later,
C.D.

Vi -
Add some work experience to your CV.
It doesn't all have to be teaching, but you did
teach as a TA here. Right?
I didn't know Noemi had accepted a ms. too.
You're doing great. None of the work
is duplicated in the self-published titles?
You can re-submit that work as ms.
Self-publishing is fine. It's takes care of the
patience stuff. But it doesn't qualify for
academic work. It dis-qualifies. And you

can send that work out in PDF form - not
the published copies. And scrap the
published copies if it gets accepted.
C.D.

vi - about to write your rec - also in academe - it is customary to
waive your right to read your rec - that is supposed to insure that
the letters are candid and can't be manipulated - so i don't know
how it works with interfolio as I've never had to write a letter before
the applicant could complete their application - but wherever that
comes up - waive your right -that would not come naturally to
you (nor would it to me but i eventually caught on that i would
be doing people a disservice if i didn't advise them of this) -
the more pro forma the better these days - academe is all
administration - it's a corporation - and this particular school -
well - it's top down on several fronts -
cd

Sylvia Plath, Virginia Woolf, Alfonsina Storni, and other famous
people who commit suicide...they travel in the underground
world.

Today Tony deleted me from Facebook. 10.12.15
And, so, as time concludes itself: my friendship with Tony has
ended. And so it is.

Everything moves unsuccessful across the landscape of time.

Signed contract with Coffee House Press.

If I were Chris Mintz I would deny that I was the hero in the Oregon shooting. I would deny up and down that I was suicidal too.

Vi Khi Later

Tofu and red tomatoes

Emmanuel gate B4 southwest 483

How did you lose yourself, Vi? How did you end up here? Where did you lose all of your self-esteem? How do I get back?

My dearest Tania, Urban Tumbleweed is, after all, urban. I checked this book out with you in mind. I read it to see if it's something you would be interested in reading. After a long steady glance into it, I have decided that you wouldn't like it. In case you felt left out: urban tumbleweed isn't what you think it is. It's, in fact, garbage bags flown out in the middle of the freeway. I guess it's as urban as it gets. And a pile of tumbleweeds of that caliber wouldn't give you the all hugs you want or desire. You had quite an adventurous year: moving across many states to be in a Catholic place called South Bend. And, with great courage, you are here with your peers, sharing an intimate part of your imagination with a group of hopefully supportive readers and friends. We use to share such an intimacy and it was beautiful. I suppose as you age you will get more and more beautiful than ever. As a result of a series of intimacies that transform you into an amazing writer that you already are. I envy your peers, as they get to sample the insightful, intelligent, delightful, and thoughtful comments you offer them weekly. I envy the ritual of coming to class, knowing that you must face something so tangibly intangible. Writing on a keyboard level is palpable, yes, but after you lift your fingers and glance into an unbearable moment called the critic, what you feel so palpable can be as ephemeral as air that wishes to become a stone. I hope this year opens endless opportunities and friendships for you. And, that you will develop a complex and immense love for the craft of writing and the craft of friendship. I hope you push yourself endlessly to create something in you that breaks the resilient parameters of what you thought you once were. Meaning, I hope you put yourself in places of great discomfort. More than that, now that you are a quarter of a century ready to bloom into another quarter, I hope you let yourself be swayed by the wind, like pastoral or urban tumbleweed. I don't know what your spirit is designed for, for you are one to grow wise very quickly, but whether you become a metropolitan tumbleweed or a dormant tumbleweed or a houseplant tumbleweed or just a weed that grows in the prairie, I want you to know that I love you and care a great deal about your happiness and well-being. You may have mistaken my silence for apathy, my arborous-like and unorthodox style of communication for stupidity, but I assure there are duck feet paddling arduously and cosmically and elegantly beneath the surface of perception as they transport a duck across the vapid, seemingly tranquil pond (hopefully not be pecked unmercifully by a prey). I hope you will have the greatest birthday you have ever imagined. Happy 25th birthday to you, dear Tania. Another tumbleweed, Vi

Latent sadness

Silence long silence

I want to clothe my mind with the thought of you—I wear everything now: clothes, ribbons, beauty, luxury.

Ke francis at ringling college of srt in darasota fj

Between hum, there is phobia.

Advance? When is the approximate publication date? Contract? Interested in publishing it with image or without image

Moving stuff to Storage from Van Anh's basement

Penis is not a salad

Noon Glimmer Train The Iowa Review Triggerfish Hobart Black Warrior Review

Happiness can make you very dishonest. It may be the beginning of dishonesty.

South Bend

I can cure your cancer with this poem, Patrick Muller

Departing Sin City

Dear Tania, The bat photographer. I will fly soon to where the cows repine in their unquiet pose. It is early. It is dark. In Sin City. The sky hasn't opened her soul yet, but I can feel myself falling asleep while the city is waking up. I am an airplane, shutting down. It is very beautiful. I believe you would love it. Even the noises of the blender or the coffee grinder can't stop the day from breaking open. We will share the same time zone soon. I am in the upper peninsula waiting for the bats to shut their eyes and for me to unleash the unknown. I wonder where your thoughts have flown. -36

Empty Mirror

In which she brought new boxers with penis flaps

Submission Party with Tania

Enemy!

Snowpiercer

Coherence

Whiplash

Breckenridge, CO

Frisco, CO

Grand Junction, CO

Coralville, IA

Moving stuff to storage with Omar.

Getting to know Omar, who is a hoarder.

picking strawberries

Mackenzie's apartment in Coralville

Writing letters to Kevin and Giovan

Camus 2011 Cabernet Sauvignon

That is what guilty people do. They get tortured by sanity.

Don't get angry until I belong to you.
Baby robins on a tractor!

Subway worker yells at me.

My mother is in love with HQCL, the solar company in Shanghai.

Adam has a flat tire.

Whores

I met Alex Lemon. He looks like Jack Nicholson. Also, he read his prose like the way he reads his poetry.

Atticus is happy!

I had a dream of my pencil. She left her husband and came over to America. She arrived with her body half in nude. Her beautiful, perfect breasts. She kissed me when she arrived unexpectedly. Then she introduced herself to Tania. I immediately found her a shirt to cover her pencil breasts and helped her put a shirt on while telling her I don't want her in jail for indecent exposure. She left her husband to be with me, but he flew to America to retrieve her. In person, the naked pencil looked smaller than her picture on Facebook. She looked exquisitely beautiful and tan. I was so afraid to be with her. She wants to help me move all of my boxes at Van Anh's place to a storage unit.

"If self-love were a mirage, it would decorate distance, shimmer over others' eyes evaporate on contact" Deteriorate ITSELF rae armantrout

Discovering lesbian work with Matt at Prairie Light!

In Iowa City

An Is Shi Vani asked, "Psychologically, what percentage of Asian are you?"

I hide all of my flowers from my friends I hide all of my tears from my family Every inch of me Is asleep in a room With clumsy boards Florentines With baklava I wish I could disconnect my flesh from my dreams My heartaches from the ethereal I wish I could dine with God On a bed of bruised plums and pumpkins so orange they make Florida jealous I wish I could wrong the neighbors several floors below Make him wear goggles left over from durian rind Instead I am left wide open like a sentence with fragments

Sheep Machine Hermaphrodite in Iowa Super clitoris Fish in Exile Old philosopher Saigon When I was Eight The Figurative Orations of Odd Nerdrum A Bell Curve The Proscenium

I don't want to eat your tongue, pencil. But I will have to. Please write a poem about Tim's belly.

EMAIL FROM LELA

Vi, ooooof, I am such a bitch. I was in transit for 2 days. Normandy is gorgeous. Lush forests, tall wispy trees, in beds of wild grass, and tiny yellow and white flowers. I want to write you so badly but I am behind on this chair.....Vi, you are amazing, moving, writing, loving, teaching. You deserve more than the words I try to give you and the ones that get lost. You gave me life, as a writer and as a me.

I hope all is well.   Are you in Providence now? Did your mail arrive?

It is hot in Phoenix the past few days. I have been reading the reviews you sent which are complex. Jeanne

It is lonely here in Providence. I don't want this pain anymore. It is breaking my heart into quarters.

East Haddam Colchester Lime Old Saybrook Middletown

East Winsor Vernon Elington The Mansion at Canyon Ridge

Charlotte's pancakes

EMAIL FROM TIM

Dear Vi,
I am so sorry, in the face of all options I took the easiest and most cowardly: silence. That seems to have been the norm for my two years in New York after college. And with it the terrible realization that I could be who I wanted to be only up to the point it became a struggle.

When you wrote me I actually was still in New York, not Japan! Working as a paralegal, very long and draining hours. I did feel overwhelmed, constantly. By you? If yes, then equally so by hundreds of others. I said I would be interested in translating your book into French, which is and will always be true. But I should have attached a million caveats, all of which would have been to say that to do so on any reasonable timeline was, at that moment, unrealistic. And faced with the consequences of my selfishly offhand commitment--your hope--I choose to ignore it as one more marker of the miserable situation I had acquiesced into, where the things I most wanted to do I was incapable of.

I'm still not wholly well, in that sense, but I am doing much better! I have made it to Japan, to quiet Kyotango, tucked between the sea and the mountains. Where once I had neighbors for five stories above me, now I live with rice fields all around. I am trying, slowly, to make my amends to those, like you, I wronged by privileging lower than corporate castigation, and to find a way for a writing practice to re-enter my life. It is still so hard! My work is much less evil on its face, but free time is taken up trying to learn Japanese and work up the energy to cook and clean. And garden, too! I have one of those now. Well, a garden of grass. Well well, a garden of weeds, truly... But my garden of weeds!

I met Stephen my last semester at Brown, in a Lit Arts workshop on OuLiPo. A lot of undergrads seemed to dislike him, which attracted me. I haven't been so in touch recently, but I made a point of visiting him whenever I was back in Providence, and once in New York he stayed with me. Last I heard he was going to the European Graduate School in Switzerland? Any more from him? The fruit, I loved the fruit. I already have plenty of psychological hang-ups when it comes to eating fruit, and that made it all the worse! And so all the better.

Vi, I hope you can forgive me my improper behavior. I plan to take a year soon to do nothing but what I please, and maybe by then I can translate your book into Japanese as well. I would very much like to know where you are, and what you are doing! Take a year to tell me, if need be. I've earned it.

Very fondly, Tim

Try to sleep for the EPIC test

Preparing for EPIC interview

Things happen so fast. The evacuation from Wellfleet!

Tolland, CT

Ruan Ji Room At Carpe Diem, Provincetown, MA

Twink—hairless, 18-23 Otter—hairy, athletic
Twink. Bald 18-23 Oreo.

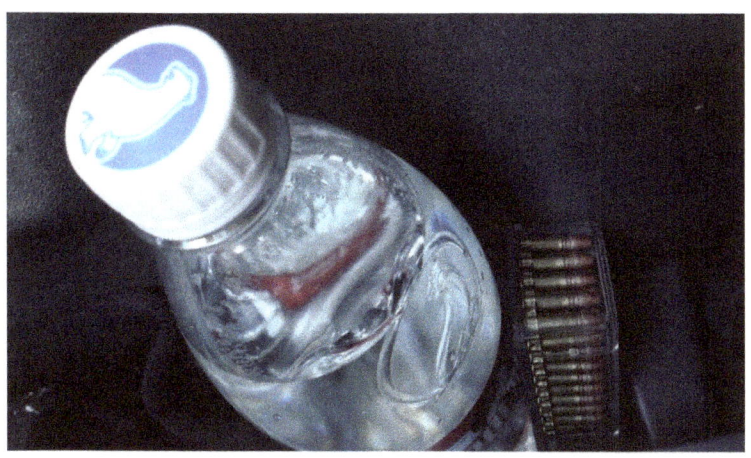

Do you think water and bullets get along? They sit together like naked nuns.

Dong congratulates me on winning The *Nightboat Prize*.

Susannah and Russell fighting over Russell's ex wife.

The wind is generous with its bitterness.

To live here at Susannah's is very lonely.

34 degrees in Wellfleet, not bad.

Russell says that the ass of the co-doula of Susannah is made of "chewed bubblegums."

Last day at Tutoring Club.

Dear Susannah,

My five words are:
1.   relinquish
2.   niveous
3.   soronal
4.   afflated
5.   commination

Returning from Sedona, AZ

Jeanne in Sedona

At the beginning of my suffering, there was lots of snow. Snow on the roof.

To break the ice, she calls us little vagina Athena.

Where has life taken me now that I am drifting? Like ice.

So many rejections in one sitting. Yale Younger Hodder.

Tania flew back home to Oklahoma on January 5, 2015. And I miss her kindness.

Last night I dreamt of my brother. My brother is making a large pot of potato soup for us. Sitting on the table alone, he chops up carrots with his hands. He tears apart the beef meat. His hands are raw. Earlier, he has made my mother a bowl of soup. This was before he threw everything into the pot. When serving my mother soup, he tosses a small airfield of salt onto her bowl. She tastes it. It tastes perfect. My sister, out of the corner of my eye, begins to overload my brother's arms with gifts, mainly twenty different kinds of chocolate, wrapped in luxurious, opulent paper wrappers, golden and bright and silvery like the stars. My brother continues to cook, rearranging the pots around the stove like ornaments on a Christmas tree.

My brother has been away from us so long. The last time I heard of him was through tin cans plucked with strings. In the same fashion as chicken's feather plucked by us. My mother heard it from my sister who rehashed it to me. My brother called my sister to ask her to transfer $300 to him so that he could fly back home. My sister denied his request. And from then on, we haven't heard from him. Every now and then, my conscience gets plucked like a guitar. A small, vibrating sound in the shape of a memory, a jotted, vacant, but charged thought of my brother, out there in the world, lonely, perhaps homeless, perhaps starving, but mainly alone, isolated, helpless without anyone helping him. And in my state of insolvency and indigence, I reach out to see how he is doing, if he is doing well, if he was dying out in the golden field of North America, at some private parking lot of God or at the entrance of a casino, tumbling from impoverishedness. No replies came from him. Not a single one. Ever since he chose to disappear from us.

Every now and then, sitting across from my mother, my mother asks the air, not God, of course not God, where is your brother? And how is he? She wouldn't ask me. I wouldn't know. My brother's addiction to gambling began when my mother's uncle's wife asks my mother if she would house her son for a couple of months. My family was then living in a three-bedroom house where six of us would share one bathroom. But my mother hesitantly agrees even though she did not want to. She hated having her privacy tainted with the familiar spirit of the unknown. But perhaps she felt indebted to my uncle in Houston. When we were refugees in the Philippines for six months, where foods were rationed to us by the ounce, my mother's uncle sent my mother's money so we could survive a little more. We had ramen noodles delivered to us in boxes. At any rate, this distant relative of us introduced my brother to the art of gambling and he became intensely addicted. He was only 14 or 16 years old, I think.

When I watched Abdellatif Kechiche's Blue Is the Warmest Color in early January in the year of the Sheep, vice is compared to gravity. How it's inevitable that it would fall. If you drop an object, it would fall. If you get your hands on vice, you would inevitably fall, like the consequence of gravity. Without going to the gym, I could lose body mass by going to the moon. My mother's relative stayed in our house rent free, food free, while he teaches my brother the art of greed, which Livermore, yes the Livermore, equates it to hope. Hope is greed, he emphasizes. So perhaps during these teenage years, my brother learned to HOPE, which is the most dangerous profession in the world. I read in an article not long ago about how gambling is the only addiction that does not enter, corporeally, the body of its host. Most addictions (sugar, caffeine, heroine, sex addictions) demand the trafficking of the skin, blood, mouth, nose, genital, but my brother's addiction is fleshless, airless, almost bloodness. Though there is a saying in Vietnamese about gambling lives in Asian blood.

The last time my brother and I are together, he was recovering from dying. When my mother divorced my father, my father bought the house next door to us. He didn't want the divorce. He fought against it and he lost. Hating her, but not bearing to be far from her, he walked three steps to his new home. Not soon after the divorce, my mother moved to Vegas, and my father confronted the emptiness of her existence. After six years, the realtor sold my mother's house. When it was sold, my mother had a living room worth of furniture from. My mother called from Vegas to ask my father if he could store them for her. He agreed. It was sometime in early Fall when my sisters and my brother and my father and I walked three steps over to my mother's house to transfer the furniture over. Against all of our advices, my brother stubbornly carried a heavy TV from the early 1990s by himself. He couldn't make the three steps to my father's house and the TV laid on the Iowa grass like a black woman in a black box bikini, tanning herself towards late winter. Eventually, my father and my sisters escorted her into my father's living room, where she would enjoy the winter in my father's lonely house. Exhausted from lifting the TV, my brother crawled back into my father's house to convalesce. Out in the yard, my father haughtily self-congratulates himself, "I am over sixty years old. Look at my strength. My son, at the height of his youth, has no energy. He is no help to anyone. Look at him. Lying in my living room."

Noticing blood in his stool, a little over a day later, I asked my sister to leave work to come over and help me transport my brother to the Emergency Room. He kept on refusing to and demanded his Gatorade. He had no health insurance. And the Obama Care would not begin for

At the hospital, my sister and my father and I play a guessing game. Who could guess accurately my brother's uninsured three-day hospital bill? My sister guessed 24K, I guessed 14K, my father 20K. When I returned home from the hospital, I brought five bottles of Gatorade for my brother. They gave him fluid, mended his hole, and he was released from the hospital. He was a few centimeters from Death. My brother didn't just come home from Florida to die. He came home to add an extra $30,000 hospital debt to his Princess Pea mattresses of gambling debt. On my phone, my mother sorrowfully cries to me, "He is destroying his body on purpose. This behavioral suicide. What to do? What to do?"

Acknowledgments:

I would like to extend my deepest gratitude to Alan Good for his unwavering support and dedication to this book. His keen eye for detail, insightful feedback, and relentless commitment to excellence have been instrumental in shaping this work into its best possible version. My thanks also go to Willow De Los Rios for her beautifully handwritten interior title, David Wojciechowski for the eye-catching, striking cover design, and Jörn Peter Budesheim for his exquisite art.

Vi Khi Nao is a multidisciplinary writer working across poetry, fiction, theater, film, and collaborative art. She won the 2016 Nightboat Poetry Prize for The Old Philosopher and the 2017 Ronald Sukenick Innovative Fiction Prize for A Brief Alphabet of Torture. Her latest novel, The Italy Letters, was published by Melville House. A former Black Mountain Institute and the current 2024-2025 Iowa Artist fellow, she was awarded the Jim Duggins Outstanding Mid-Career Novelist Prize in 2022.

Poetry Collections

The Old Philosopher (Nightboat Books, 2016)
Umbilical Hospital (Press 1913, 2017)
Sheep Machine (Black Sun Lit, 2018)
Human Tetris (11:11 Press, 2019)
A Bell Curve Is a Pregnant Straight Line (11:11 Press, 2021)
Fish Carcass (Black Sun Lit, 2022)
War Is Not My Mother (Clash Books, 2023)

Fiction & Nonfiction

Fish in Exile (Coffee House Press, 2016)
A Brief Alphabet of Torture (Fiction Collective Two, 2017)
Swimming with Dead Stars (Fiction Collective Two, 2022)
The Italy Letters (Melville House, 2024)
Suicide: The Autoimmune Disorder of the Psyche (11:11 Press, 2023)
The Vegas Dilemma (11:11 Press, 2021)
The Vanishing Point of Desire (Fugue State Press, 2011)

Cross-Genre & Collaborative Works

Waiting for God (Apocalypse Party, 2022)
Human Tetris (co-authored w/ Ali Raz, 11:11 Press, 2019)
The Six Tones of Water (co-authored w/ Sun Yung Shin, Ricochet, 2024)
That Woman Could Be You (co-authored w/ Jessica Alexander, BlazeVOX Books, 2022)
Funeral (co-authored w/ Daisuke Shen, Kernpunkt Press, 2023)
Timber & Lụa (co-authored w/ Lily Hoang, Red Hen Press, 2025)
Mechanophilia (co-authored w/ Sarah Burgoyne, Anvil Press, 2023)

Also Available from Malarkey

and Death of Print

Kill Radio, a novel by Lauren Bolger
The Barre Incidents, a novel by Lauren Bolger
Faith, a novel by Itoro Bassey
The Life of the Party Is Harder to Find Until You're the Last One Around, poems by Adrian Sobol
Hair Shirt, poems by Adrian Sobol
Music Is Over, a novel by Ben Arzate
Toadstones, stories by Eric Williams
Deliver Thy Pigs, a novel by Joey Hedger
It Came From the Swamp, edited by Joey Poole
Pontoon, an anthology of fiction and poetry
What I Thought of Ain't Funny,
edited by Caroljean Gavin
Guess What's Different, essays by Susan Triemert
White People on Vacation, a novel by Alex Miller
Your Favorite Poet, poems by Leigh Chadwick,
Sophomore Slump, poems by Leigh Chadwick
Man in a Cage, a novel by Patrick Nevins
Fearless, a novel by Benjamin Warner
Don Bronco's (Working Title) Shell, a novel?
by Donald Ryan
Un-ruined, a novel by Roger Vaillancourt
Thunder From a Clear Blue Sky,
a novel by Justin Bryant
The Muu-Antiques, a novel by Shome Dasgupta

Malarkeybooks.com